Published by:

S.C. Fitch Enterprises Publishing

20650 Matteson Dr., Suite 445

Matteson, IL 60443

Cover design:

Sandra Ballenger

www.sandraballenger.com

Sandraba@msn.com

Edited by:

Christine Clukey Reece

Christinecreece.wordpress.com

ACKNOWLEDGEMENTS

If you'd asked me a few years ago if I had any thoughts or goals of being an author, I would have told you, "No, it's never crossed my mind." It didn't until my best friend, Coach and Speaker Da-Nay Macklin, called me one day. She was excited about joining an organization for authors and speakers, and she was impressed with an awesome lady in that organization — *Erika Gilchrist (The Unstoppable Woman)*.

Da-Nay told me she was participating in Erika's new literary project, where 24 women would contribute to a unique guide for women that covered numerous subjects and issues. She mentioned that the financial chapter was not taken, and then asked me if I'd be interested in applying to write that chapter.

My husband wrote a book a few years ago, so I decided to challenge myself and go for it; after all, it was only one chapter. I am so glad I did! Now I am a contributing author (Chapter 20) to the awesome book *The Unstoppable Woman's Guide to Emotional Well-Being.*

After previously writing to share financial knowledge, this time I decided to write about something more personal — and something that I am more passion-ate about. I am eternally grateful to my best friend

Da-Nay for your unwavering friendship, mentoring, and encouragement, and for introducing me to Erika. Thank you for sharing Erika and this wonderful achievement/milestone with me! Erika, I thank you for being a coach, mentor, and friend to me. You two ladies truly inspired me to be Unstoppable.

I would also like to thank Dr. Anthony Gantt for his continuous encouragement, guidance, and mentorship.

I'd like to send out a special thank-you to my "Mini Me," Jazmine, for inspiring me to continue to grow as an example of what you can accomplish with hard work and determination. I love you, and I'm proud of the young lady you are becoming.

Lastly and most importantly, I'd like thank my husband, Steve Fitch, for always supporting my many endeavors and for always loving me and being my rock. I also thank you for creating our first personal Erotic Cookie Jar, a gift that keeps giving! Our love and continuous effort has inspired me to share our strategy and help others to keep the fun and spice in their marriages.

INTRODUCTION

When you see veteran couples (folks older than 40) or elderly couples (folks older than 60) being romantic in public — i.e., holding hands, kissing, dancing, having dinner, etc. — do you sometimes find yourself pondering the following questions?

- How long have they been together?
- Are they still physically intimate?
- How the heck did they stay together so long when so many other couples are getting divorced left and right?

I know I have. As a woman who has been married for over 20 years, I can tell you it takes a LOT of work on six key things:

1. PATIENCE
2. COMMUNICATION
3. FORGIVENESS
4. THOUGHTFULNESS
5. LOVE-BASED EFFORT
6. SEXUAL AND INTIMATE EXPRESSION & COMPATIBILITY

Trust me, you'll get bored, want to kill each other, and often want to trade each other in for a new model.☺ Luckily, my husband and I have navigated through those times, coming through the other side and loving each other more than ever. We're both blessed to have a spouse that does all of the things listed above and more. We use the first three key elements to get us through the issues and troublesome times, and we use the last three to make the good times...*oh so SWEET!*

This book focuses on #6, Sexual and Intimate Expression & Compatibility. We'll go on a romantic, erotic journey into many ideas and experiences that will help fellow veteran couples, and newly established couples, keep the fires burning in their love lives.

Table of Contents

CHAPTER 1:

~~~

THE INCREASING NEED FOR THE EROTIC COOKIE JAR

~~~

You may be wondering what a Cookie Jar has to do with my love life and why we need it. Well, let me explain the correlation.

You may have heard the term "Cookie" most recently in Steve Harvey's book *"Act Like a Woman, Think Like a Man"* (one of my favorite books, a must read). In his book, Steve explains why it is wise for a woman to give a man she's dating a 90-day probationary period before giving up the goodies, referred to as the "Cookie."

This has been a popular nickname for a woman's loving and/or related parts through the ages, and I'm so glad Steve has made it popular again. My hubby and I have old-school tendencies at times and we've used the term for years in our intimate conversations.

My husband has always been thoughtful and creative when it comes to romancing me, so it was a natural thing for him to invent the Erotic Cookie Jar — a cookie jar full of romantic fantasies — as a playful way to spice things up.

After using the Cookie Jar for several years with great success, we shared the idea with several of our friends and colleagues (those who dared to share that they sometimes fell into the same romantic slump that we occasionally experienced). In time, we received wonderful feedback and were elated to hear the juicy success stories.

We decided that if this concept was so successful for us and for many others, it was something we had to share with the world. Many couples just need something sweet, fun, and spicy to go from fizzle to sizzle.

What Happened to My Sexy Partner in Crime?

When most couples start dating, the chemistry is so thick you can cut it with a knife. They think about each other all day, every day, and they try to spend time together every chance they get. In most cases, the man will move heaven and earth, even traveling across town in a blizzard or on public transportation, to get to his love. Sometimes he'll even do so just for a short stolen moment or a quick kiss.

The woman will often pull out all the stops to make sure her man always sees her at her best. If she knows he's coming, she will rush to put on something sexy, fix her hair, put on her favorite perfume, and get her face right. She does it all to get that wonderful reaction from her man, seeing him gaze at her in awe and hearing him say, "Damn, Baby, you look good," and maybe even seeing him bite his bottom lip with hopeful thoughts of ripping her clothes off later.

I remember two movies in particular that perfectly capture this feeling. In the movie **Pretty Woman**, do you remember when Richard Gere sees Julia Roberts for the first time after her stunning makeover for their first real date? Or even better and more recently, in the movie **Act Like a Woman, Think Like a Man**: remember when aspiring chef Dominic (Michael Ealy) sees his executive diva crush Lauren (Taraji P. Henson) come out of her condo building for their first date? That feeling is PRICELESS!!!

After the initial wow moment, you and your sweetie will go and paint the town red. If things go well and you click, you'll become inseparable after a few weeks. As your comfort level with the other person grows, you find yourself going everywhere together and experimenting with all kinds of sexy escapades.

Your mate is not only your road dog, but also your sexual partner in crime. Think back to a few times when you and your current (or past) lover did something wild and crazy...something that makes you blush when you think about it, or better yet, would make your mother say "What the hell?!" if you told her. I'll wait...

(pause)

Yeah, those moments. Matter of fact, to make sure you never forget, make a cryptic note in the space below of your top three "Lord, forgive me for sinning but that 'Ish' was Off the Chain" moments (as the young folks would say). I say cryptic because you may or may not want people to know what you are referring to if they happen to pick up your book. The best way to do this is to use initials or a key word that will jog your memory and help you re-live that moment.

Trust me, this quick trip down memory lane will make you smile and get your head in the right place to take in the ideas in this book. For the sake of fairness, and to show that I won't ask you to do anything I'm not willing to do myself, I'll go first. Mine are:

1. S & S
2. LMO
3. I C E

All I can say is OOOH & WEEEEEE!

Okay, I'm back…. Now list yours:

1. _____

2. _____

3. _____

Are you smiling, or should I say smirking, yet? I know that I am after writing those down. I'm sure you may have much more than three of these moments —I know I sure do. If so, that's fantastic! It means you've tapped into your erotic side.

Believe me, everyone has an erotic side, even the super saints. Yes, even saints and super Christians, Muslims, etc., have had moments that they had to say an extra prayer about to God.☺ If you are feeling slightly offended because I may be referring to YOU, don't be. It's really okay! Remember, no little saints got here because people were on their knees in prayer!

The real problem is if you can't come up with at least three of these moments. If you can't, you haven't tapped into all of the aspects of being human. God made us with three key life motivators: **Intellectual, Emotional, and Sexual.** Most things we do in life initiate because of one of these motivators.

Intellectual: what we think, know or learn

Emotional: how we feel about something or someone

Sexual: our natural erotic response to something or someone

If you can't come up with three WOW moments, you haven't really tapped into all aspects of your soulful life experience. After reading this book, I'm sure that you'll find an experience or an idea that intrigues you enough that you'll want to add it to your life experience. Most of us would love to experience moments like these on a regular basis with the one that we love. Unfortunately, after time passes in a relationship, the desire to wow each other with our looks, charm, and efforts just seems to fade away. We let that crazy thing called LIFE get in the way.

The sexy man, the one who used to make sure he had a fresh haircut & shave and smooth threads, used to say and do all the right things to make you swoon. Now he sits around the house in sweats, torn jeans, or khakis, and with some ugly shirt he found on the floor in the closet. Maybe he's glued to the game on TV, or he's off with his buddies, helping with religious activities, working 50 plus hours a week, or coaching a game somewhere as soon as he gets off work.

This issue goes both ways. The same can happen with the lovely woman who used to wear sexy dresses or shirts, fitted jeans, leggings, and miniskirts. She laughed at your jokes and enjoyed going dancing and doing many activities with you — including the naughty ones. Now she just wants to stay home and watch TV, or only do activities with the kids, her girls, the church, or her social group. *She* may even be the workaholic.

Nothing is wrong with these things, and you may even admire them in your man or woman. However, when these things get in the way of your time for romantic or sexual interludes, your relationship can have a problem. You two used to go everywhere together, but now it's hard to find any time for fun, romance, and love. Now all of your time and energy focuses on your career or the kids.

This lack of special time coupled with the "I already got him/her" syndrome (meaning, "I don't have to put effort into impressing my mate or proving my love anymore") can have a major impact on your relationship, and it often leads to infidelity. This is a road that no one wants to go down, but it is a very real possibility because people have a natural desire or need to feel special to someone. More often than not, if someone's mate doesn't inspire that feeling, the person will seek it with someone else.

I'd like to share a testimony from a friend of mine:

> My wife and I were the best of friends while we were dating and the early years of our marriage. We went everywhere together...ball games, trips, pool halls, racing tracks, motorcycle riding, clubs, etc. Oh how we used to close many clubs together. We both loved to dance and would stay on the dance floor all night. We were together so much, folks used to ask where our shadow was if they saw only one of us somewhere.
>
> After my wife had our 2nd child, everything changed. She no longer wanted to go anywhere. And I mean anywhere — not even church. She said that she didn't have time for childish things anymore; we had to focus on the kids now.
>
> Now I expected our outings to be scaled back now that we had children to raise, but I didn't expect that we would have to stop living altogether or that I would lose the funny, sexy, outgoing person that I married. We didn't even talk, laugh, and joke around like we used to. Everything was so serious, or if things were light and cheerful, unless it was child related. Now some folks may say that she

may not want to go out because she gained weight with the pregnancies, but that is not the case. My wife is still gorgeous, especially to me, so I don't get it. I would often offer to help more around the house or to get a sitter so that we can have a date night, and she would always refuse. She just sent me out with my fellas. My going out alone, or with the fellas, all the time often put me in very compromising situations. Most of the time, I was able to avoid doing something that I'd regret later. One time, however, I was feeling particularly down and did not handle my frustration of being out alone, and I befriended a lady I met at a sporting event I attended with my fellas. After a period of time, we became very close and our friendship turned intimate. I unfortunately ended up getting caught and hurt my wife very badly. I know that there was no excuse for my actions, and I am so blessed that my wife considered both sides of the breakdown in our intimacy.

During this time, I confided in Cynthia, and she shared with me some things she and her husband did to rekindle their spark when things became a little mundane. She gave me tips on how to set up a sacred recurring block of time for us and blessed me with the secrets of her Erotic Cookie Jar. After implementing some of her ideas, we worked things out and are now stronger than ever. Now we make sure that no matter what our responsibilities are, we find a way to carve out some "US" time.

Believe it or not, my wife and I both realized that our kids seeing us still romantic and into each other makes them feel secure. They are able to survive a day or night without us. This year, we will be celebrating 12 years of marriage. Thank you so much!

–Chris X

I wanted to share my friend's story with you because I know that he is a wonderful husband, father, friend, and man. Even the best folks you know, who have the best intentions, can have a lapse in judgment when intimacy breaks down in a relationship. Spending quality time with your loved one and finding ways to enjoy each other in and out of the bedroom is crucial to any long-lasting relationship. It is NOT an option, folks — it is a MUST!!!

We are all human. We all make mistakes, but if you believe you are with your best friend, then you should be willing to do most anything with, to, and for your mate. Remember that once you're married, you can have other friends, but your mate is the only one you are supposed be intimate with — your commitment is to please each other because that other person is IT until you die or divorce.

Having hang-ups about pleasing your mate is cruel and abusive, and it's why some people consider marriage to be a death sentence. Don't do this to your marriage. When you say "I do," you should be okay with loving your mate from head to toe. Literally! You didn't get married to be bored, or to take care of just your own sexual needs; you and your mate should be sexual partners in crime.

You shouldn't feel ashamed about anything you and your mate enjoy doing. Don't worry about someone judging you, just shut the heck up and enjoy what you enjoy. Got it?

My husband and I have been married for over 20 years, and we're just like any other couple — we have our good days and rough patches. We have periods in which we take each other for granted and maybe get a little bored. This is bound to happen in any long-term relationship. One thing is for sure: no matter what dilemmas may come our way, we are both determined to be part of the 50-Years-Plus Golden Couple Club. This is what we all should strive to achieve.

Many folks ask us how we keep the fire burning after so many years. I often simply say we are still dating each other. This means we still do silly, fun, freaky stuff like we did back in the early years. You can do this too!

With that said, let's dive into the next chapter to find out more about the Erotic Cookie Jar. It helped us (and our friends!) deal with this common, but serious issue in a fun and mysterious way that kept the spice in our love life.

My goal is for this book and the Erotic Cookie Jar to be the perfect gift for any man or woman who is falling in love, in a loving relationship, married, etc., to enjoy — and to use to keep the smiles coming and the fire burning. I want every couple that truly loves each other to have the ability to reach Golden status.

CHAPTER 2:

PREPARING FOR THE EROTIC COOKIE JAR CHALLENGE

This chapter will prepare you to take a romantic journey and introduce some great ideas into your love life. Most romance books target women, and for good reason. Many of us are hopeless romantics at heart and need an escape to the love life we wish we had. However, men can benefit by learning the types of erotic thoughts we have, and about the right things to do to bring out that side of us so that both parties can be sexually and intimately fulfilled. This book speaks to both men and women about ways to explore some amazing romantic dates and fantasies, whether big or small, easy or complicated. It will keep you both asking, "What's in your Cookie Jar?"

This romantic journey combines general ideas with specific details, and even some personal experiences from me — and from couples who were gracious enough to share some of the moments that still make them smirk when the memories cross their minds.

DISCLAIMER:
I realize that my readers may be in different places in their spirituality, so please consider the fantasies when you reach a point where you feel comfortable implementing the ideas. For my super saints, some of these ideas are great for after you are engaged, and others may be more applicable when you finally say those beautiful vows...and then IT'S ON!!!

The Erotic Cookie Jar is a romantic tool that helps to create mystery, excitement, and romantic and sexual fulfillment in any relationship — if used correctly. It is a romantically designed cookie jar with flavored fortune cookies that open to reveal a romantic fantasy challenge, which can fulfill one of your loved one's most romantic and erotic desires if carried out. Cool idea, right?

Imagine how you would feel to know that within the next few days, your sweetie would do something that would definitely put a smile on your face, and ultimately lead to what I like to call a G.G.N.

(Guaranteed Good Night). I'm sure you will look at your mate a little differently over the next few days as you anticipated his or her interpretation of the fantasy challenge and how it will be would carried out. I know I sure did. Just thinking about should bring a big smile to your face.

You and your mate can decide how you want to regulate the use of the Cookie Jar. By this, I mean that you decide when to pop open and select from the Cookie Jar. You can choose to set a date periodically to do it, perhaps on a special date night. For example, if you generally go on a regular date night at least every other Friday, then you can make those Friday date nights your Cookie Jar nights as well.

For a frequency option such as this, you can elect to give the person 48 hours, 72 hours, a week, or until the next date night to complete the selected fantasy. Now if you choose to use the Cookie Jar more spontaneously, you can just use it when either of you feel that things need a pick-me-up — or when you are just in the mood to do something spicy.

NOTE:
With this timing option, I would recommend giving each other a 48-hour deadline after you select a cookie from the jar.

Now there are exceptions to the rules for some of the fantasies. As you will read in some of the following chapters, some of the fantasies require planning, preparation, and funds for purchasing required items or securing reservations at certain romantic spots. For these fantasies, all you need to do is to communicate to your mate that you need a certain amount of time to fulfill the fantasy. Make it a reasonable time-frame — like a week, tops.

NOTE:
Once the challenge is over, you share the fantasy sheet with your mate to show you carried out the task.

There is only one firm and non-negotiable rule for the Erotic Cookie Jar. The rule is that you absolutely MUST carry out the fantasy on your sheet. This rule is in place to ensure that both sides receive excitement and enjoyment from this relationship-enhancement tool, knowing that new and exciting things they have desired will soon come to pass with the one they love.

With this firm rule, I also include a pre-established deal-breaker clause. This alleviates the panic someone may feel when thinking about his or her mate taking advantage and asking for a deal breaker. For example, one person may be opposed to threesomes or anal play while the other might be very curious about experiencing it. This phobia is a reality for many couples and is understandable; however, people may have phobias about other things that are worse to them, and they may be okay with these ideas.

Everyone has different phobias and different curiosities, so the deal-breaker exercise is necessary and required preparation for using the Cookie Jar tool. You must put your love and understanding in the forefront and not judge your partner's desires. Just decide if it's the top deal breaker. Over time, you may be able to work out the other ones as you grow together.

You'll establish this clause together before you pull out any fantasies from the Cookie Jar. I want you to challenge and push yourself, so I will only allow two deal breakers per person. Think hard about the one or two things you absolutely will not do under ANY circumstances. Remember that this is the person you decided to spend your life with, so there shouldn't be too many things you would refuse to try with them — even if the things seem weird to you.

Think of it this way: if you are the ONLY person this person is supposed to be with intimately for the REST of their life, wouldn't you want to be the ONLY person that they would ever even think about going to in order to fulfill their fantasies? Your mate should not be scared or embarrassed to share any fantasy idea with you. Bottom line: if you are IT for the rest of that person's life, you should be okay with saying, "Baby, if you want to do something that feels good to you... I got you", (as long as it doesn't hurt you)! ☺

The best and most fair way to set this up is to start with the following steps:

1. Write down the one thing that is an absolute "NOT gonna happen, come hell or high water."

2. Now write down the next two things that make you really uncomfortable and that you'd prefer not to experience in your life.

3. Now determine which of those two items seems worse to you.

4. Make the worst one of those two your second deal-breaker clause.

Okay, now you have your two Cookie Crumblers (deal breakers). I'm sure you must be curious about that third item, since you don't plan to do that either. That third item is your "I'm not ready to even think about that" item. The reason I'm not making it a deal breaker is because I really want you to push yourself... but not until after you've spent several years successfully enjoying all the other fantasies you never thought you'd explore together.

Remember that the levels of romantic activities in this book will be at varying levels of sexual comfort. While some things may seem trivial and very basic and make you go "duh," other things may make you say, "Aw hell naw, who the hell would do that?"

Please remember to try to take in the ideas without judging them. There may be some things you're not comfortable trying now. Several years from now, you may become intrigued about the fantasy or it may even be second nature. Trust me, after many years of marriage or being committed partners, many couples become comfortable with exploring things they'd never have dreamed of trying early on in their relationships.

Think about it — and let's be frank. There was a time when people thought oral sex was appalling. Now we would think someone was crazy if they said they didn't feel comfortable doing that with their mate, especially if they were married. Let's agree to keep an open mind and have some fun. Okay?

Each of the following chapters will reveal cookie challenges from the Erotic Cookie Jar that will offer a fantasy for you to explore, (I'll share how to customize your own Erotic Cookie Jar challenges later). The chapters will contain a mixture of recommendations on how to carry out a Cookie Jar fantasy and some stories of how others carried out their challenges. These stories come from various sources: friends, family, Facebook, online blogs, and chat rooms. I've switched or altered some of the names in order to maintain the privacy of my fantasy sources.

You don't necessarily have to use what I recommend or follow the stories verbatim unless you want to do so. It's just a guide to get your creative juices flowing. The fun part is that you don't know what's in store until you open a cookie. By the time we are done, you may want to add a few of your own fantasies to your jar. I'll also share with you how you can order customized Cookie Jar Challenges.

Let's start exploring some things you may find in the Erotic Cookie Jar!

LOVE

ROMANCE

SEX

ADVENTURE

CHAPTER 3:

MEALTIME FUN

Do you remember when you were a kid and your parents constantly scolded you for playing with your food? Those days are over, and you're grown up now. Who says it's wrong to play with your food, especially with your mate? In fact, it can be sooo right!

Let's say one of you pulls out an Erotic Cookie Challenge that says, ***"Find a sexy and creative way to share a meal with me."*** Here are a few ways you can pull that off:

Spaghetti Slurp Fest
Being romantic sometimes means letting your inner child out and just having fun. Have you ever seen the

movie *Lady and the Tramp*? As a child, I thought that it was the most romantic thing in the world when Lady and Tramp ended up sharing the same strand of spaghetti. They almost kissed; their lips almost touched as they met at the center of the long pasta strand. This idea or something equally simple might be perfect way for a novice or conservative couple to carry out the challenge.

I have other ideas for my more experienced and sexually adventurous couples, including a personal story you may want to explore if you haven't already tried this. ☺

Chinese Surprise

It was a very long day for Charlotte's husband. He called her several times just to hear her voice. The last time he called, near the end of the day, she asked him what he had a taste for in the way of food. He paused and said, "I think I'm feeling like Chinese food tonight." She said, "Cool, I gotcha." She wanted to make sure that when her hubby got home, he could eat and relax that evening, and then maybe later she could do something to put a smile on his face.

Charlotte expected her hubby to home around 6pm, but at 6pm, she unfortunately got a phone call from him. He said that he had to work a little later and wouldn't be home until 7:30. She was a little disappointed because she was a bit hungry and wanted them to eat dinner together. She decided to heat up a little food, just to hold her until he got home. While heating up her food, she got a bright idea: "Why don't I feed my hubby his Chinese food from the sexiest plate I can think of...ME."

She called her hubby a few times to get a gauge on what time he was going to get home from work. She asked if he was hungry, and he said, "Famished." She smiled and said "Good." She told him that she'd ordered a special Chinese meal for him, and in order to get it, he had to follow all of her directions. He smiled through the phone and said, "Yes, ma'am."

I'm sure I don't have to tell you that he finished up at work rather quickly. He followed her directions and called her when he was leaving, and then called again when he was two minutes away.

She then heated up his favorite Chinese dish just enough so that it was warm, but not hot enough to burn her. Just as she heard him pulling into the garage, she took off her clothes and laid on the dining-room table. She took the food and spread it from her neck to her belly button. When he opened the door and saw the super-hot and sexy meal she'd prepared for him, he dropped his bags, threw his coat off, quickly ran to washroom to wash his hands, and then sprinted to the dining-room table to enjoy every inch of his meal!

Dinner Is Served

There is nothing like working all day and coming home to a hot meal, especially when your mate is nice enough to make up your plate and serve it to you. The only thing better is having it served by a super-sexy waiter or waitress. You could wear a lot of different sexy things to make this fun.

Women, you can go Hooters-style and wear a tight T-shirt or tank top with Daisy Duke shorts; you could also wear lingerie, or go all out and get a waitress costume. Guys, you can wear a tank top and shorts, a sexy tight or netted shirt, no shirt and shorts (or biker pants), a waiter's costume, or just a robe. I like the last option best.

It may even be fun to role-play this challenge. Give your mate the menu, grab a note pad, and pretend to take your mate's order (the woman can lean over to show cleavage, and the man can make sure his sexy chest or package is at face level). After you take the order, let your mate get comfortable. Seat them and serve them their wonderful dinner while flirting with them and hinting of the evening to come if they are a good boy or girl.

To add extra spice, be sure to feed your mate the first bite. If you join your mate in eating the meal and you feel really frisky, you can consider "accidentally" dropping some food down your shirt, on your chest, or on your lap, and then ask for help getting it off (wink!).

When your mate finishes eating, take their plate seductively while rubbing your body against them, and then take their napkin and gently dab their mouth and plant a soft, seductive kiss. Ask if they enjoyed dinner, and then whisper softly in their ear that they will love dessert.

Make sure dessert is something fun to share, or something messy that you'll need to clean — I mean lick — off. For this, I recommend making a sundae with strawberries, chocolate, and caramel, and topping it off with whipped cream. My favorite is alcohol-infused whipped cream (it comes in several yummy flavors).

Hot Momma Sundae
If your Cookie says you have to be creative with a meal, who says the meal can't be dessert? Fellas, here's a creative and somewhat popular way to do dessert. Gather some strawberries, bananas, and caramel and/or chocolate syrup. Personally, I think caramel is best because you can slightly warm it and it's a little more sticky, which means you need to put a little more effort into getting it off.

Cut up the fruit in small pieces. Prepare a nice cozy spot where your sexy lady can lay down. Then commence to making your masterpiece.

Note:
You may want to consider using a blanket you don't mind messing up. You may also consider cover a sheet or blanket with a plastic tablecloth.

To add a little extra spice, use alcohol-infused whip cream. This nicely flavored whip cream has a kick, and you can purchase it at most liquor stores. It comes in flavors such as caramel, raspberry, chocolate, cappuccino, etc. Oh — don't forget to place a cherry on top of whatever spot you choose. ☺

Big Daddy's Banana Split

Ladies, if you like bananas and whip cream, you can do something similar to the Hot Momma Sundae for your man. Take all of the ingredients previously mentioned (or add or change up whatever you like), place the dessert wherever you choose on your Big Daddy, and eat it up. For those who are very freaky, or should I say sexually comfortable? You can eat up the banana pieces, or omit them altogether and focus on decorating Big Daddy's banana and cleaning him up in your own special way. ☺

YUMMMMM! That was a delicious chapter, wasn't it. Now let's move on the exploring with you mate outside of the house.

CHAPTER 4:

TAKE IT ON THE ROAD

One of you pulls out a Cookie Challenge that says, *"Take a chance and find a creative place away from home to make out with me."* The options for this challenge are limitless. Here are a few ways you can fulfill this fantasy:

Picnic for Two

When was the last time you went on a picnic, just the two of you? There is nothing like being out in the elements, feeling the wind blowing in your hair as you relax among tall, beautiful trees — or even better, resting beside a beautiful lake, river, pond, or ocean. Listen to the beautiful sound of rushing water hitting the shore as you sip glasses of your favorite wine — it's a sure bet to get you both in a romantic mood.

Say that one of you pulls out a cookie that challenges you to **"Plan a romantic picnic for two in a beautiful location."** The first thing you should do is inform your mate that this challenge could take some time to plan, and ask your mate to give you a week. Be sure to complete the task in that time-frame unless a major tragedy occurs.

I recommend keeping the meal light. Include finger sandwiches, cheese, crackers, a light salad or pasta salad, your favorite fruit, and *please* don't forget the chocolate (if you like chocolate) or your favorite light dessert for that sweet tooth. I highly recommend chocolate-covered strawberries because you can have fun feeding them to each other. Last, but not least surely, don't forget a bottle of your mate's favorite wine, or mood-altering drink of choice. ☺

Now, let's take this wonderful, common romantic outing and spice it up a little. Ladies, nothing spices up a picnic more than if you wear a sundress or wrap skirt with "<u>no</u>" undies underneath it. Not only will you get to feel free and enjoy the fresh air (and occasional refreshing gusts of wind) ☺, but the reaction you'll get when your mate rubs on your butt, (either accidentally or on purpose) and notices you're bare will definitely make both you smile.

If this happens, fellas, you must put your big britches on and rise to the occasion. The worst thing you can do is to reprimand your mate for being so daring, or to not be daring enough yourself to let her know that you appreciate the bold gesture.

If you are at all puzzled on what I mean, then shame on you. But just in case, I'm saying to be bold enough to spend some time on that picnic feast, using your fingers or whatever else you dare to use on her bare assets, to show your appreciation. Ladies, if you have a super-shy mate that did not get the memo, you may have to be bold. Put his hand on your va-jay-jay to jump-start the fire.

Once the fire starts, what makes things spicy is the threat of being seen by someone. Have fun, but try to be discreet. The worst-case scenario is that a park ranger will catch you. Anyone else who sees you will either say "Get a room" or cheer you on, snicker, or just act like they didn't see you, especially if they are on the same mission. ☺ Just enjoy the moment...it's worth it. Years later, you both will look back on it and smile because you were able to check that off your bucket list.

Pull Over Before You Crash

Keeping the fantasy of taking it on the road in mind, have you ever gotten hot and bothered while in the car with your mate? Perhaps you were on the way home from a wonderful date and your mate put you on Cloud 9. You got the urge to show them just how happy and turned on you were, and it just couldn't wait until you made it home. So what do you do? You decide to kiss and begin rubbing on your mate, and eventually tug at their pants.

We've seen the "make out session while rolling" scene periodically in comedy shows and movies as a sort of joke. I'm sure at least a few of us have wondered "Is it illegal to perform fellatio while your mate is driving?" I would imagine so, especially since drinking or being intoxicated, talking on your cell phone, and texting are all illegal. If done correctly, I think this would be the most distracting thing of all for a driver.

Come to think of it, I do know of a case where a woman was giving her lover fellatio while he was driving, and he ended up going off the road and dying in the crash. She was charged with homicide. I'm pretty sure that if you cause an accident doing this, you will be in quite a bit of trouble, especially if your actions result in serious injury or death.

For my more adventurous couples, if this is a fantasy you would like to scratch off of your bucket list, listen up. The best way to carry out what is probably most men's fantasy of getting head while driving is to softly whisper while tugging on his pants, "Pull over, dear, before I make you crash." Then after he pulls over to a safe location, handle your business! ☺

Hhhmmm, what a chapter! Now lets get on over to the toy store.

CHAPTER 5:

PLAY TIME
YOUR TOYS OR MINE?

One of you pulls out a Cookie Challenge that says, ***"Find a sex toy for us to explore together."*** For my veterans, this means find a new sex toy to explore.

Toy Intro Party
I once attended an Erotic Toy Party. Where a few guess attending turned their noses up and were offended by most the items there, although everyone knew what type of party it was. Being shy is understandable, but being offended was surprising. Heck, I found myself blushing at some of the high tech gadgets. Unfortunately, they were so obvious

with their judgment and disgust that they made the presenter and most guests feel uncomfortable.

From this experience I learned that sexual exploration with toys is not for everyone, but please know that using them does not make you a bad person. Finding out that you are aroused by toys can be an amazing observation that only enhances your sexual experience. It doesn't hurt it and can be a simple substitute when you mate is not around.

If you are a novice, try starting out with something simple like a heated massage cream or a waterproof vibrating bath sponge. The sponge is a great idea because it can inspire you to make time to take a romantic bath together. After cuddling, talking, soaking, bathing, and sharing some quality intimate time, there's nothing like a vibrating sponge to give you both that jolt to get you out of that tub and on the better things rather quickly. ☺

Scavenger Hunt

When you were a kid, did you ever experience an Easter Egg Hunt or a Scavenger Hunt? Do you remember feeling the thrill of the chase and the anticipation of what you might find in various hiding places, especially when the prize was an awesome toy or yummy candy? Go ahead and re-live those feelings in a grown-up setting. The following is an idea that either person can carry out. It can also be fun for both the person setting up the hunt and the one on the hunt.

Picture this: you come home from another boring day at work. After parking the car, you walk to the garage door and see a sign, that says; "This will be no ordinary night…. If you follow all of my instructions, use your imagination, and follow my clues, there is an awesome surprise waiting for you! Go inside, set your bags on the floor by the door, take off your coat, then head to the closest place to wash your hands."

You go to the bathroom that is right next to the garage door, and there you see a note that says, "Wash your hands and take me to the place where I cut up all of your fruit." You go to the kitchen and look on the island, where you see a small casserole dish covered with foil. It has a note that says, "Put this in the microwave for two minutes, and go to the place where you prep that sexy smile each morning."

You go upstairs to your master bathroom, and on the sink is a gift bag with a note that says, "Take off your clothes right here, freshen up, and put on only what's in the bag." You open the bag to find a sexy loungewear (something you both were recently eyeing at your favorite store), and a bottle of her favorite cologne for you. When you open the box for the cologne, there is another small note that says,

"Grab the bag again, and then go to where you lay your head."

You go to your bedroom and lift up your pillow to find a large feather, a blindfold, and a note that says, "Go to where you keep your drinks cool." You go to your kitchen refrigerator, which holds a chilled bottle of your favorite wine. It has a note on it that says, "Take the dish out of the microwave, and bring us and the bag of goodies downstairs to where the smoldering light dances."

You take all of the goodies, head downstairs, and walk toward the lit fireplace in the family room. There you find your beautiful lady with nothing on but a long red scarf and high heels, or you see your sexy man with nothing on but a tie and boxers. Your mate is lying on the floor on top of several plush blankets, surrounded by refreshing finger foods, and holding a final note saying: "Dinner is served!...Hungry?"

Sex Dice

Our friends keep a pair of sex dice on their bar as a conversation piece. These always seem to evoke an interesting conversation at every one of their parties. Why? Well, if you don't know what sex dice are, let me tell you. They are dice where one die has a command, such as kiss, fondle, lick, etc., and the other die has a picture or description of a body part, such as lips, ear, breast, etc. There is also a different version where one die has a picture of a sexual position and the other die tells you what room in the house to do it in.

I highly recommend purchasing this fun little toy to keep in your nightstand. They are very inexpensive and offer a great return on investment. You can usually find them at romance/novelty shops or online for around $5.

Besides being an amusing conversation piece, they can be a very fun and erotic tool in the bedroom. You and your mate can decide to designate a specific day, week, or month as "Dice Day." You each get to roll the dice five times throughout the day, and the other person has to do whatever you roll.

If you don't want to know it's coming, you can add "Dice Day" as a custom Cookie Jar fantasy for your mate: *"Roll the sex dice five times and do whatever you roll to me before you go to bed tonight."*

Looks like every roll will be a win-win! Don't you agree?

So, what do you like to do in your spare time? What do you do to just get away from it all, a movie, read, video game? Next, lets explore some hobbies couples can enjoy together.

CHAPTER 6:

HOBBY TIME

It's game time! Let's look at some of the ways you can use games and hobbies to create sexual intimacy with your partner. Let's say you pull a cookie jar fantasy that says, ***"Find a way to turn one of our hobbies into a G.G.N. - Guaranteed Good Night."*** Here are a few ways you can accomplish this:

Halftime Fun with Sexy Sports Wear
The next time your man's plans to watch the game with the fellas falls through and he ends up having to watch by himself, ask him if he minds if you watch it with him, at least for the first half or second quarter. During the first quarter, make sure he has all the food

and drinks he needs so that he's comfortable and in a good mood. Be sure to have on your sexiest sports gear with no bra and super-short shorts. Tell him you have a surprise for him at halftime.

As soon as the whistle goes off for halftime, give him a quick moment to see the replay of the last major move of the game, then quickly straddle him and maul him with kisses. Open or lift your shirt, put his head between your breasts, and proceed to get him aroused. Once you accomplish this, and if you are comfortable enough, give him mind-blowing head or ride him.

As soon as you hear the whistle for the game starting back up, just stop abruptly and kiss him gently.

Whisper, "Enjoy your game," and walk away. Trust me, he will want to continue the halftime activities sometime later after the game, if he even lets you leave the room, especially with DVR's now a days ☺!

Warning:
Be mindful and careful about doing this during a major game that he's 100% committed to watching. I would recommend doing it during the "B" game of the day — the one before or after his favorite team plays. Please don't take it personally, if you don't get the response you are looking for immediately. He may not respond as planned, but believe me you planted a seed!

Sexy Sports Bets
There are many other ways you can turn a sports activity into a romantically fun night for the two of you. Use your imagination to create more situations and other ways to use game time. One huge tip I will share is, that even if you don't like sports, learn the basics of your mate's favorite sport anyway.

This is a GAME CHANGER, ladies. Believe it or not, your mate will appreciate the effort, and it can allow you to spend more quality time together doing something your mate really enjoys. Now you can occasionally watch games with your mate and make sexy bets on the plays or the final score, (i.e. a certain halftime score gets a juicy kiss...or something more—hint, hint).

Another idea is to learn to play a sports video or arcade game, and to make sexy bets on the outcome when you play against each other. This can work with any sport: football, basketball, golf, soccer, etc. Use your creativity to come up with bets you'll both enjoy!

Dancing the Night Away

Dance is a seductive art that releases natural endorphins that can put you in a sexy state of mind. Even if you are not the best dancer, I highly recommend dancing together — whether it's in the privacy of your home or out on the town. You can use date night to take lessons to learn a style together, such as Salsa or Stepping (or Steppin, depending on whom you ask). Stepping is a form of ballroom dancing that originated in Chicago. It's lots of fun and can be very romantic. Here are a few links where you can learn about Chicago Stepping and its romantic magic.

Google:

Six Brown Chicks Chicago Style Steppin

Snoop and Crew

YouTube:

Steppin' with Bruce

Dave Maxx & Rhonda Freeman

Who says partying at home can't be sexy? Here's a cool example of how you could sizzle and dance the night away at home if you don't want to go out. Check these videos out!

YouTube:

Victor James & Nicola Thomas Steppin Again

Two Steppin Kansas City Style January 26, 2011

If these styles are too slow for you and you prefer something less structured, I recommend Reggae or Housing (simple rhythmic dancing). See the following sites to get an idea of House music and dancing.

YouTube:

Frankie Knuckles Boiler Room NYC DJ Set

OLDSKOOL HOUSE - 89 90s - MIX

House Countdown(Chicago TV show-1990)

Pump Up The Volume:
Part 1 - The History Of House Music

HDDD Episode 5:
House Dancing in Chicago Outside The Warehouse

How to Dance Up on a Girl | Sexy Dance Moves

For these styles, you just move to the beat — no judgment and no instruction needed, just move.

I realize that some couples may not be comfortable going out to clubs. Perhaps you had a bad experience, or an incident during a previous relationship. Here are a few things to consider so that you can ease your mind and have fun.

Identify your insecurities and discuss expectations with your mate! Before going out to a club with your mate, get a hold of your feelings and fears. Ask yourself the following:

- *Am I nervous about my mate dancing with another person?*
- *Am I okay with other people speaking to or having casual conversations with my mate?*
- *How would I handle it if someone hit on my mate?*
- *How would my mate handle it if someone hit on me?*

If you have any worries regarding the answers to these questions, address them with your mate.

Remember that when you are out partying, it's okay to be sociable. Just be sure not to be disrespectful. Decide what your boundaries are, how to handle questionable situations, and your methods for dealing with other people at the club. By doing this, you can both enjoy the experience of being out together and having fun with each other and with other people.

I would also recommend bringing mutual friends from time to time. This way, you can mingle primarily in your group, which can increase your fun and reduce the chance of uncomfortable incidents. The goal here is to have fun. Believe it or not, the atmosphere at a club can sometimes enhance the reasons why you fell in love with your mate in the first place — maybe because they are fun, friendly, or even a great dancer. The wonderful thing about dancing is that even if you aren't the best dancer, you can use your physical closeness to brush up against each other and whisper sexy things in your mate's ear. After dancing and flirting the night away, you are almost certain to end the night by continuing to dance — between the sheets!

Paint a Sexy Picture

If you or your mate is into art, you can turn this hobby into a romantic time as well. Painting and wine parties are starting to become very popular. This is a party where people and the materials to paint a picture come together, along with some appetizers and wine or another beverage of choice. A few friends of mine have attended them and said they're a lot of fun. You can attend one together and paint a picture of each other, or go alone or with your friends and bring home a picture and present it to your mate.

If you want to do something more personal, you can ask your mate to pose for you (with or without clothes, if they're daring enough) so you can paint, draw, or photograph them.

If you're not an artist, do a sexy photo shoot with your mate or for your mate. There are many reputable photographers and companies that offer glamour shots, where you can have them take a dressed up or sexy picture of you. Present it to your mate as a gift. You could also have a private photo session at home with just the two of you. Just whip out your camera and take your own sexy pictures. Be sure to agree on what to do with the pictures after you've taken them, and respect your mate's wishes.

You can also consider creating a scrapbook of your best dates and include thoughts of how you felt about your mate at that time. Mention the sexy, bad, or nasty things you wanted to do or did that day.

Implementing any of these creative ideas together can help you turn that hobby into a special time where you can reconnect physically.

Hope you learned some now ideas about hobbies the two of you can do together. Now let take the hobbies, and prior things you learned in prior chapters and elevate your day to day chores.

CHAPTER 7:

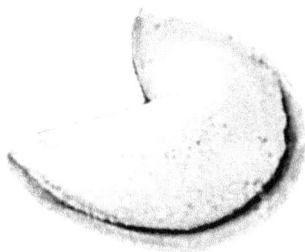

REDEFINING HOUSEHOLD CHORES

Household chores definitely keep many couples at odds, mainly because the woman often carries the burden and feels like she can't get any help. What if you can add a sexy element to the chores so that there is nothing but smiles at the end of the rainbow. Wouldn't that be fantastic?

Let's say one of you pulls the Cookie Challenge to ***"Find a way to seduce or tease me while completing your household chores."*** A simple way to pull this one off is to wear something sexy while you work. This can mean anything from wearing a cut-up T-shirt and some short-shorts, to cleaning in your lingerie or one of his shirt, or for an extra effect add high heels or even a pair of feather pumps.

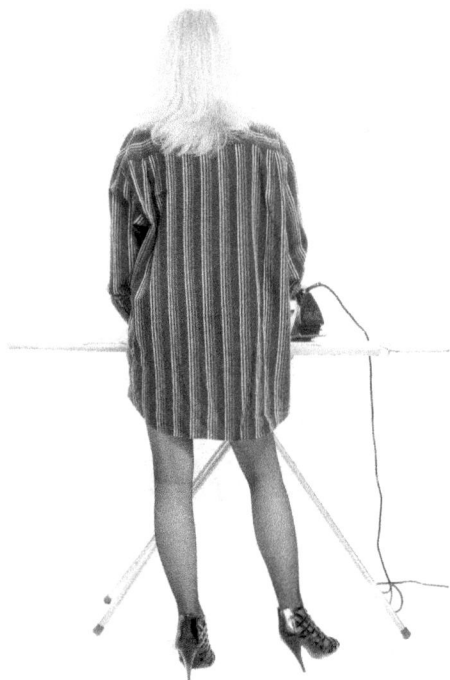

Note:
Men actually love when women wear their shirts.

Guys, you can do your chores in sexy mode too. There is nothing sexier than watching a man cook, clean, or do yard work with no shirt on or in a nice-fitting "wife beater." Ladies, you *know* what I'm talking about.

When you do this, the key is to kiss or grab a body part on your mate every time you pass them. If you really want to stir things up, and you are feeling good that day, try doing your chores in the nude when it's just you and your mate in the house. Alternatively, do your chores first in your clothes. When you are almost done and you know your mate is on their way home, jump in the shower and do the last little final tasks in the nude after they arrive.

Be sure to greet your mate with a big ole sloppy wet kiss. Keep doing subtle things to tease your mate while cleaning, like constantly bending over, reaching past them to grab stuff, etc. If you do this one right and your mate has a clue...you should end up thrown up against a wall and manhandled, or pushed onto a table or over a chair (or couch) and worked over thoroughly!

This reminds me of a story one of my former co-workers shared with me a few years ago.

Kristy was always coming to work complaining about her lazy husband. She often referred to him as her "Lazy-Ass Man." She constantly fussed that she had to do everything around the house, from the cooking and cleaning to yard work, and she often had to take out the garbage too because he kept forgetting and she couldn't take the smell.

No matter how much she complained, he would only do one or two things to shut her up, and then just fall back into his old habit. He'd come home from work, take his clothes off and throw them on the floor, and then plop on the couch. He'd just ask for his dinner and veg out for the evening.

This used to totally piss Kristy off, especially since she was working a full-time job too. She was so frustrated and tired that sex was often the last thing on her mind. She was always angry and tired, of course, and this made her husband (Carl) resent her because they'd started their relationship as a very sexually expressive couple. Now she had to deal with a sexless marriage on top of being overworked and over-stressed.

I shared the Erotic Cookie Jar idea with her, and at first, she was very reluctant. She said, "Girl, thinking of creative things to do with him sexually is the *last* thing I want to do." I replied, "But what if it's not just you having to come up creative things to do? This challenge is for both parties, and trust me, you both will benefit."

She agreed and tried it out. Just so happens that Carl pulled out the challenge that said, ***"Find a way to seduce or tease me while completing your household chores."*** Carl surprised Kristy — he showed up and showed out!

On the day he decided to carry out his challenge, Kristy came home to a sexy stranger in the kitchen. Her husband was at the sink, washing dishes in nothing but boxer shorts. Not only was he doing the dishes, he had some food cooking on the stove.

Kristy was stunned. She gave him a big wet kiss and asked him what he needed her to do, and he said, "Just go get comfortable, I got dinner tonight." She said, "Aww, sooki-sooki now," and went upstairs to put on something sexy.

When she got back downstairs, he sat her in his lounge chair, gave her the remote, and said, "Just relax, I'll be in back in a minute." Then he kissed her gently on the forehead. She got chills up her spine and thought to herself, "Who the hell is this man?"

She watched him in the kitchen, preparing their meal like he was a pro. He looked up, saw her staring, and gave her a little smirk. Then he flexed his oil-covered chest, which make her instantly hot. "Dang, he hasn't done this to me in years," she said to herself.

After a few minutes of her watching this sexy stranger, he came over to her and poured her a glass of her favorite sparkling Moscato. He even went through the trouble of placing a strawberry on the rim of her glass. When he bent down to give her the drink, she couldn't help but start rubbing the soft hair on his chest.

Carl gently grabbed her hand and placed it on his erect cock. She felt a rush hit her privates. Just as soon as he put her hand there, he removed it, and then put the glass in her hand instead and said, "Take a sip, no worries, he will definitely see you later." Bewildered, she just sat there, trying to pretend she was looking at the TV, but periodically staring at the sexy stranger who'd taken over her husband's body.

Within a few minutes, he returned to her side and knelt down next to her with a plate of King Crab legs with warm lemon-butter, twice-baked potatoes, and steamed asparagus. She was beyond stunned! She reached for her utensils, but he stopped her and said, "No, dear. I got you." He then proceeded to crack the crab legs and take out all the meat for her.

He fed her the first piece and basked in the look of ecstasy on her face, followed by a sensuous hum of pure satisfaction. He then sat beside her and prepared his food, and they sat and ate and talked like they hadn't done in years. After dinner, she rose to take the plates, but he stopped her again, grabbed the plates himself, and took them to the kitchen.

While he was at the sink prepping the wash water, Kristy couldn't help herself. In one split second, she glided into the kitchen, pinned him up against the sink, got on her knees, and gave him the best head since the day they got married. They then proceeded to get it <u>ON</u> all over the house, from the kitchen to the dining room to the living room.

She came back to work the next day with this story and gave me the biggest hug. She said, "Girl, there is something to be said about adding a little sex to your chores." Balancing the chores in their house made a serious shift for the better.

So who's ready to do some housework? Next, I'll share some tools of how to handle your work-a-holic.

CHAPTER 8:

~~~~~~~~

WORK ME, BABY!

~~~~~~~~

What on Earth am I going to do about that workaholic of mine? I realize that times are hard and the bills keep piling up, but can I get a minute of your time, please? Hello... starving husband/wife here! Yooohoooo, remember me? Ever since my mate got that darn job and/or promotion, I can't get a minute in edgewise.

Do any of these questions or statements sound familiar? Please know you are not alone, not by any means. Nowadays, in this steadily declining economy, many of us spend an enormous amount of time trying to keep our heads above water, not to mention trying to get ahead. Many couples fall victim to these issues at one time or another, just like so many other couples do.

Back in the early 90s when I was working crazy hours at a top CPA (Certified Public Accountant) firm and studying for the CPA exam, I had *workaholic* stamped on my forehead. After a long day of working and studying, I only had time to eat, study, and sleep when I got home. Luckily for me, we didn't have any kids at the time. Spending time with my hubby was the last thing on my mind, not to mention anything else.

I remember us going weeks without eating a meal together. By the time we were both made it to bed at night, I was snoring before he could even raise his hand to reach over and touch or rub me.

Scenario like these are unfortunately the reason many couples end up in an infidelity crisis. When the workaholic issue is short lived, usually due to just trying to meet a deadline or complete a project, most couples are able to weather the storm without any issues or major temptations. However, when the issue causes a lack of intimacy for a long period of time, the door is open for vulnerability, and not everyone is as strong as they think they would be in this situation.

So what can help keep the intimacy intact when one person is carrying a heavy load and has difficulty fitting in time for their loved one? I'll share with you some things I've learned to mastering the art of the quickie date! Yup, sometimes quality is more important than quantity. If your mate doesn't have a lot of time, then steal a few moments here and there and make the most of it.

Here are a few suggestions that worked for us and for some of our friends who also endured what I like to call "An Overworked Marriage":

Love Notes
When there isn't a lot of time to spend together, it sometimes helps just to know that your mate thinks

of you. Imagine you were disappointed that you couldn't spend any time with your mate all week because they were working. One morning, you might wake up and find a sticky note on your bathroom mirror that simply says, "Just wanted you to know that you are always on my mind, and I love you very much."

It would make your whole day shine. You could also consider putting a love note in your mate's briefcase, purse, or lunch bag.

This simple expression of love can make anyone's day and possibly give them the encouragement to push past an obstacle. If you are lucky, that boost of energy may push them to finish up early and come home to show their gratitude.

Power Lunch Break
There are two different ways to get the most out of lunchtime:

1. Pick up your mate's favorite meal, take it to your mate's workplace, and surprise them with it. If your mate is super busy and doesn't usually have time to take a full lunch break, you may want to call ahead. Give them a head's up and get a good idea of the best time to pop in to see them. The worst thing that can happen is for you to go through all that trouble, but not be able to see

your mate to steal a kiss or chat for a few minutes because you stopped in while they were in a meeting or on a conference call with a client. Your mate may be appreciative, but your effort will not have the result you wanted, and this may cause you to be even more resentful.

If your plan goes well, then hopefully you will be able to surprise your mate with lunch and spend a few moments, either in their office, lunch area, or outside, and steal a few smooches and a little touchy-feely while eating.

2. If you desire, you can turn **#1** up a notch. The hope here is that your surprise goes VERY WELL, and you are able to REALLY enjoy your lunch time together. Here is an example of taking it up a notch:

One day while Lisa an aspiring attorney and self proclaimed workaholic who never leaves the office for lunch. The night before she mentioned to her husband she was craving the jumbo shrimp for the restaurant a few blocks from her job. The next day her hubby surprised her with a shrimp dinner for lunch. She was quite surprised and happened to be horny. No one was really in the office that day, so after a few smooches, one thing led to another, and well...you know. It was like something out of the movies. Luckily they managed to only knock a few things off her desk!!

After-Office Hours
What could be better than a hot lunch? A yummy after-hours surprise at work can make working late a wonderful experience. Just imagine this: You're working really late — say 8:30 or 9:00 pm — and you're the only poor soul stuck in your office. Your mate calls to check on you and finds out that you are hungry, but you don't want to stop to get anything so that you can hopefully finish and leave there by 10 or 11 pm.

An hour later, your mate shows up at your office with dinner for you. How appreciative would you be? What if they didn't just bring dinner, they also brought dessert? By this, I mean your mate showed up in a long coat (preferably a trench) with sexy lingerie or biker shorts and no shirt underneath. They have a quick bite to eat with you, jump your bones, then politely get up, kiss you goodbye, and say, "Now get back to work...see you at home later," and vanish.

Elevator
I got this idea from a friend, and the best way to share it is to just put it in a story.

Candice was working late yet again, and couldn't pick up her sweetie from the airport. He flew in for the weekend for a family gathering, but his first plan was to see his lady. When he landed, he called Candice to see if she was near the airport. She reluctantly told him that she couldn't get away. Her boss had loaded an assignment, on her before leaving for the day, that was due the next morning. She was up for a promotion, so she couldn't say no.

He was disappointed, but didn't say anything because he didn't want to bring her down any more — he could definitely hear sadness and worry in her voice. He simply said, "Don't worry, I can catch a cab. I'm stopping by the office to see you on the way to my mom's, is that okay?" She sighed and said, "Yes, that would be great."

Next, he asked what she was wearing. She said, "A skirt and a sweater." He said, "Great, I only have one request...take off your underwear." She said, "What! Are you kidding?" He replied, "No, just do it for me, please." She agreed.

When he showed up at her building, she had to take the elevator down from the 15th floor to open the door for him. He greeted her with a kiss and a dozen roses, and what he did next blew her mind. They got into the elevator to head up and with one quick motion, he pinned her up against the wall, lifted her skirt, knelt down, and went to town. She was so shocked, she couldn't speak.

As soon as they reached the 15th floor, he got up without saying a word, walked out of the elevator, and went to her office. She just stood there with a dazed look on her face, thinking, "Damn...*what* has gotten into him?" I'm sure you can guess that the rest of their weekend was eventful!

"Work" Sign

Okay, I've had it! My hubby was downstairs in his office working at 7:30 this morning, and now it's 10:00 pm. He's been working like this for the past three weeks, and I'm horny, dammit!

If you find yourself in this situation, this next idea is one of my favorites. If it doesn't work, just beat the hell out your mate!!!

Just kidding... don't do that. But seriously, if you are a little bold, give both of you a treat the next time your mate is buried with work all day. Take a shower, and then find a piece of paper, get a marker, and write the word "WORK" on it in big letters. Try to fill up the piece of paper. This way, your mate can't say they didn't get the message.

If he's working in a room nearby, you can yell out, but if he's downstairs in the basement, grab your cell and call him to say, "Babe, please take a quick break and come here. I need your help with something." If he asks what, repeat to him, "Just come here, please." Now keep in mind that your mate may be a little disgruntled if he was in the middle of something, but if he's got half a brain, the risk on this move will definitely pay off. When you hear him coming up the stairs, shut the bedroom door, jump on the bed facing the door, lay down, and put the "WORK" sign between your legs. My hubby couldn't do nothing but laugh and say, "You are a fool!" Well, I tell you one thing...he took a nice break. ☺

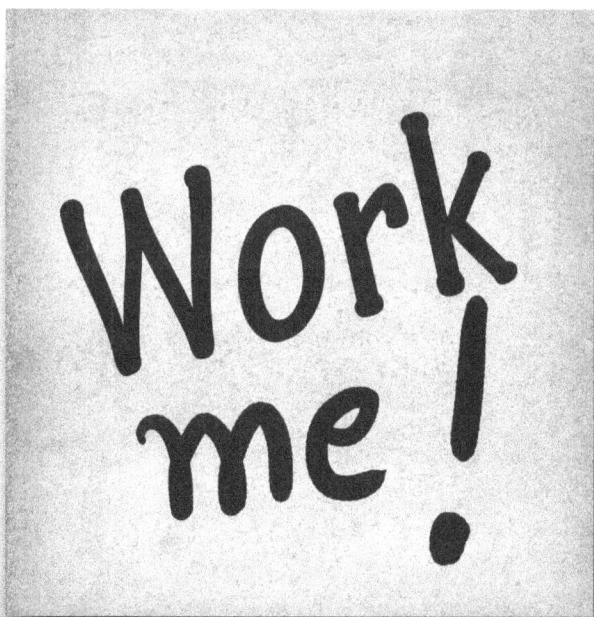

<u>Note</u>:
Fellas this idea can workout well for you too.
Now that work is done, let's go back to having
even more fun. In the next chapter, we'll use your
imagination to stimulate your relationship.

CHAPTER 9:

LET'S PLAY PRETEND

One of you pulls out a Cookie Challenge that says, ***"Be a big kid and play pretend by transforming yourself into a character or a room into a fantasy place, then seduce me."*** As children, we spent countless hours pretending that a room in our house was a fantasy place we saw on TV or in our dreams, or we pretended we were some awesome character and found whatever we could in the house to transform ourselves into that role.

Indoor Picnic
Another twist on the picnic idea is to take it indoors. On several evenings, either my husband or I have

surprised the other with a romantic picnic for two right in our family room. You can transform a room in many ways; for example, you can put candles everywhere or turn on the fireplace, and then put a blanket on the floor, spread flowers on the blanket, and have your meal there.

If you don't have a fireplace, be creative and purchase a fireplace or beach scene via software to put on your TV so you can pretend you're at the beach. For an added touch, surround your blanket with plants to give your space a tropical outdoor feel. You could also consider changing your attire to a tank top or sexy T-shirt and super-short or loose shorts.

Be sure to include a game to play while you're picnicking that will result in your clothes coming off. My recommendation is trying Poker or the Twister game. There is nothing like ending the night with a game of Strip Poker or Naked Twister.

One-Night Stand

I'm sure if you asked ten women if they've had or would have a one-night stand, at least nine of them would say "No" and at least five of them would say "Hell naw!" Believe it or not, according to Datingadvice.com, approximately 36% of women and 59% of men nationwide have admitted to having a one-night stand.

Having unknown lovers is dangerous. With diseases on the rampage, and the possibility that the person could end up stalking you (we all know how that could end), I definitely would not recommend a one-night stand with a stranger.

There is a type of one-night stand that I HIGHLY RECOMMEND. It's one with your mate. Yep, I said it: with your mate. Please note: this challenge is only for my experienced and secure couples. Now I'm sure you are thinking, "I've been with them lots of times, how can I have a one-night stand with my mate or spouse?"

Well, let me paint a picture. Make a pact to go out one night, but arrive separately and pretend you are not together. If you want, you can pretend to be strangers or that you're old friends who just so happened to end up at the same club or event. You both should mingle and chat with other folks, and if you are veterans, even have a cocktail or dance with someone else before coming together.

This may seem awkward for couples who are more conservative, but I challenge you to push yourselves. Think of it this way: most people tend to think their mate is more appealing when they realize someone else finds them attractive. Believe it or not, it may actually help your mate feel sexy and become a bit more playful if they know that they've still got "IT." Don't worry, though —you'll end up with the prize. You will be perfect recipient of all of that newfound confidence and playful sexiness later.

Just remember to keep your interactions with other people somewhat brief; i.e., only one or two dances and only one drink. Be sure to tell the person that you're meeting someone there soon, but don't mind dancing or having a quick drink to be sociable. This is key.

Now the fun begins! After mixing and mingling with other folks at the party or club, one of you comes up to the other and says hello. Give each other a friendly hug and complement each other on how nice the other looks. This is the kickoff for your date. From this point on, you two will spend the rest of the evening talking, flirting, drinking, and even dancing if you so choose. The goal is for you two to have a good time together, with the chemistry so thick between you that you can't wait to get home to rip each other's clothes off.

Once you decide it's time to leave the club, whoever pulled the pretend card should suggest that y'all continue date at home with a night cap. Upon agreement, you'll leave the club together. Once you make it inside the house, quickly grab your mate, pin them against the wall or the door, and begin kissing them passionately. You know what comes next! Your

GGN – Guaranteed Good Night. There you have it: a successful, acceptable One-Night Stand!

As you wipe the sweat off your fore-head, take a deep breath, because the next chapter is for the grown and daring. Are you ready?

CHAPTER 10:

~~~
## *I DARE YOU*
~~~

If there's one thing I've learned in my 40 plus years of life, is that men love a challenge. They especially love a good challenge when it comes to women, and more specifically, a woman they are attracted to and/or love. Women love a challenge too, but our challenge is more to obtain *and* maintain love, affection, respect, romance, intimacy, and have mutually gratifying sex for the duration of the relationship.

Now that you have had just a taste of the ideas and fantasies that can be part of your reality by taking the Erotic Cookie Challenge, I dare you to start doing things differently. I dare you to add more fun, excitement, adventure, passion, spontaneity and romance to your relationship.

If you are one of my more advanced couples that have done many of the simple suggestions noted in the book, I dare you to push yourself and your mate even further, or to repeat the things that gave you great pleasure —with a new spin, of course! One great thing about the journey of the Erotic Cookie Jar is that no matter where you are on the sexual spectrum, you can find many things to do that you haven't yet done, find different ways to do something that you have done, or just be reminded to continue doing the things that work for the two of you.

After being married for over 20 years we, just like other long term committed couples, are constantly looking for ways to keep our friendship, communication, intimacy, sexual exploration, and overall relationship constantly growing and evolving. We know that we are not the same people we were when we got married at ages 21 and 22. We technically grew up together and endured many situations that might have ended other relationships. We both had to choose to do the following:

1. Determine what are our deal breakers were and understand that those could change as we evolved as individuals and together as a couple.

2. Be candid with each other, even when it was difficult to hear or accept.

3. Not judge each other based on society's standards.

4. Truly understand who the other person was (and is), and love them because of their strengths and despite their shortcomings.

5. Allow each other a certain level of freedom and privacy.

The tip I would like to share is agree to just have fun, live life to the fullest and push each other buttons, but in a positive manner. Be sure to focus from time to time to get back to what got you two together in the first place. I like to call this the foundation. If you two loved to dance, continue to dance like no one is watching. If you love to draw. Draw yourselves a picture of love until you are out of ink... but do it together. Whatever the foundation is in your relationship, getting back to that always works wonders.

In short, talk...talk...talk!!! Remember communication is one of those things you two did constantly in the beginning. Remember those conversations that went on all night until one of you went to sleep. ☺

In addition, the two of you have to be open to discuss various topics and decide what is comfortable for the two of you, but remember that you have to open your mind and expand your horizons. An important fact in talking about uncomfortable things is to keep it in a non-judgmental fashion, and do not make it personal. The bottom line is... you are not in this journey alone. If you accept a lifelong commitment to someone, one of your direct responsibilities is to please that person intimately and sexually. You must push yourself to grow so that your relationship does not feel like a prison sentence.

One of the most common complaints that I receive from both men and women is that their spouse will not do or even attempt the thing that gives them the most pleasure. Mind you, I'm not talking about anything truly racy like a threesome, but more basic things that provides them with pleasure, like oral sex, full body massages, including rubbing, caressing, and kissing their mate's feet. (Especially the toes.)

Note:
Manicures are crucial for a treat like this.

If this seems gross to you, keep in mind that you pledged your devotion to that other person before God. If your spouse the only one who is supposed to be intimate with, then you should know every inch of that person's body. You should know what makes them tick, what gets them off, and what makes them holler!

My husband and I have committed to dare each other to do something simple each day that improves our sensual communication, adventure, intimacy, or sexual exploration, and our overall bond. I challenge you to start right now!

Just like many of our couples who will read this book, we have done quite a few things in the book and beyond. However, I wanted the book to pique your interest and help remove some concerns or barriers for those of you who have them, and to let you know that it's okay to really let your hair down with your spouse and/or life companion. The Erotic Cookie Jar is a mixture of simple things to explore or repeat and some serious challenges that will make even the most sexually advanced couples blush. We tried to create fantasies for every taste.

I hope you will join us and take the Erotic Cookie Jar Challenge starting today. You didn't think I would ask you to do something we weren't doing, did you? ☺

I'll leave you with a few simple dares to add to your daily or weekly challenge. Mix them up — and then add your own!

I DARE YOU TO...

- *Sext (aka text a dirty message) your mate.*

- *Give your mate a wet, powerful kiss the next time you are in an elevator alone.*

- *Make out on the beach.*

- *Don't wear underwear on your next date, and whisper this fact softly in your mate's ear while you're out and about (provided it's not freezing outside).*

- *Have or go to Karaoke night and sing a love song to your mate.*

- *Sit in the back and make out with your mate the next time you go out for a movie (like many of us did in the early years).*

- *Threaten your mate with a sexy promise if they do X, and carry out the promise.*

Lastly, I DARE YOU TO...

Purchase and use the Erotic Cookie Jar, take the challenges, and send me your feedback within two months. You'll receive a special prize!

ABOUT THE AUTHOR:

Cynthia Fitch, CPA

A unique and vibrant woman who wears many hats: financial manager, entrepreneur, park commissioner, wife, mother, mentor, and award-winning author. She is an honor's graduate from Chicago State University with a Bachelor of Science in Accounting, and she has attained many awards and certifications over the years, including being nominated and included in The All- American Scholars Collegiate Directory, The Outstanding Young Women in America Directory, the Financial Executives Institutes Academic Award, and SPAA's Author of the Month Award.

By day, Cynthia is a registered CPA in the state of Illinois and a seasoned professional with over 18 years of experience in the accounting and auditing sector, focusing on financial auditing, internal audits, and compliance auditing for several notable CPA firms, including the former Big 6 firm Arthur Andersen. She also dedicated a considerable portion of her career to financial management for several major corporations, as well as the non-profit sector. She even did a short stint as an instructor at Sawyer College (IN), where she taught Principles of Accounting and Business Math.

Cynthia is also the President of S.C. Fitch Enterprises, Inc., which provides financial and operational consulting for small to mid-size businesses and audit assistance to CPA firms. The company owns and publishes Amateur Sports News Network, an online media magazine that covers youth athletics in the Chicagoland area.

Cynthia and her husband are now adding another business segment to the company, focusing on relationship enhancement through self-published books and products. They both believe that marriage does not have to be boring, and that it can be a fun lifelong adventure if partners communicate and make a concerted effort to improve the sensual communication, adventure, intimacy, and sexual exploration in their relationship. Their goal is to help as many couples as possible join them in their quest to be part of the 50-Year-Plus Golden Marriage Club.

In her spare time, she enjoys cooking, traveling, dancing (Stepping, Line dancing, House, Salsa, etc.), listening to live bands, relaxing at the beach, and mentoring teens, and most recently has developed a passion for writing.

Cynthia previously co-authored The Unstoppable Woman's Guide to Emotional Well-Being (released in January 2012), contributing the financial chapter entitled "Your Map to Financial Prosperity". The book can be purchased on Amazon or through Fitch's corporate website at **www.SCFitchEnterprises.com**.

This time around, she wanted to write about something more personal and fun to help bring romance and excitement to as many couples as possible. She hopes readers will join the Fun Couples Club by going to **www.TheEroticCookieJar.com** to purchase and take the Erotic Cookie Jar Challenge.

Cynthia's life motto is, "Live everyday like it's your last, and do your best to fill the dash." We are all born and must eventually die — fill your dash with as many unforgettable moments as possible that give you a natural high!

I DARE YOU TO TAKE THE EROTIC COOKIE JAR CHALLENGE!!!!

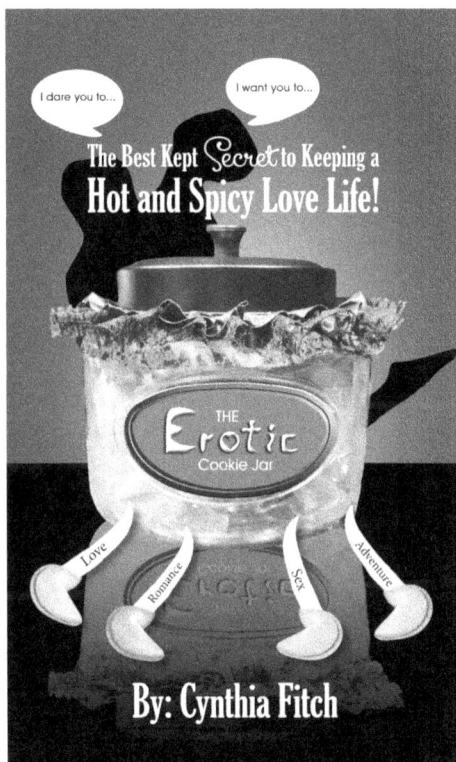

"I can't wait to hear how the Erotic Cookie Challenges have rekindled and kept the SIZZLE and SPICE in your love life!"